BABY BEANIES
Made with the Knook™

Knooking is the new knitting!

These sweet little baby hats are a joy to create, because the exciting new Knook makes knitting fun! The Knook is a specialized crochet hook that creates true knitted fabric, while the attached cord completely prevents dropped stitches! Clear instructions on the basic technique start on page 30, and are included for both right-hand & left-hand stitching, while photos illustrate each step! You'll also find excellent videos at LeisureArts.com showing how simple it is to get started.

Get more! Visit LeisureArts.com for additional Knook pattern books, easy instructions, and our clear how-to videos! Look for the Knook at your local retailer or LeisureArts.com!

TABLE OF CONTENTS

LEISURE ARTS, INC.
Little Rock, Arkansas

BUMPS

 EASY

Sizes

Sizes	Finished Circumference
Newborn to 3 months	10" (25.5 cm)
3-6 months	12" (30.5 cm)
6-12 months	14" (35.5 cm)

Size Note: Instructions are written for size Newborn to 3 months with sizes 3-6 months and 6-12 months in braces { }. Instructions will be easier to read if you circle all the numbers pertaining to your baby's size. If only one number is given, it applies to all sizes.

MATERIALS

Light Weight Yarn 🄳
[5 ounces, 360 yards
(141 grams, 329 meters) per skein]:
  1 skein
Knook, size G (4 mm) **or** size needed for gauge
Marker
Tapestry needle

GAUGE: In pattern, 22 sts = 4" (10 cm)

Techniques used:
• tbl *(Fig. 2, page 26)*
• K2 tog *(Figs. 7a & b, page 28)*
• P2 tog *(Fig. 12, page 29)*

HAT

Ch 53{65-75} sts.

Foundation Rnd (Right side)**:** Bring first ch around to meet last ch made, making sure that the ch isn't twisted and pick up a st in the first ch and in each ch around *(see Circular Knitting, page 26)*. Place a marker to indicate the beginning of the rnd: 54{66-76} sts.

Rnds 1-5: (K1, P1) around.

Rnd 6: Purl around.

Rnd 7: (K1 tbl, P1) around.

Rnds 8 thru 27{31-31}: Repeat Rnds 6 and 7, 10{12-12} times.

SIZE 3-6 MONTHS ONLY
Rnd 32: P 15, P2 tog twice, P 28, P2 tog twice, P 15: 62 sts.

Rnd 33: (K1 tbl, P1) around.

Rnd 34: P2 tog twice, P 12, P2 tog twice, P 22, P2 tog twice, P 12, P2 tog twice: 54 sts.
Rnd 35: (K1 tbl, P1) around.

SIZE 6-12 MONTHS ONLY
Rnd 32: P 17, P2 tog twice, P 34, P2 tog twice, P 17: 72 sts.

Rnd 33: (K1 tbl, P1) around.

Rnd 34: P2 tog twice, P 14, P2 tog twice, P 28, P2 tog twice, P 14, P2 tog twice: 64 sts.

Rnd 35: (K1 tbl, P1) around.

Rnd 36: P 14, P2 tog twice, P 28, P2 tog twice, P 14: 60 sts.

Rnd 37: (K1 tbl, P1) around.

Rnd 38: P2 tog twice, P 12, P2 tog twice, P 24, P2 tog twice, P 12: 54 sts.

Rnd 39: (K1 tbl, P1) around.

ALL SIZES
Rnd 28{36-40}: P 12, P2 tog twice, P 22, P2 tog twice, P 12: 50 sts.

Rnd 29{37-41} AND ALL ODD NUMBERED RNDS thru Rnd 37{45-49}: (K1 tbl, P1) around.

Rnd 30{38-42}: P 11, P2 tog twice, P 20, P2 tog twice, P 11: 46 sts.

Rnd 32{40-44}: P 10, P2 tog twice, P 18, P2 tog twice, P 10: 42 sts.

Rnd 34{42-46}: P9, P2 tog twice, P 16, P2 tog twice, P9: 38 sts.

Rnd 36{44-48}: P8, P2 tog twice, P 14, P2 tog twice, P8: 34 sts.

Rnd 38{46-50}: P2 tog twice, P5, P2 tog twice, P 10, P2 tog twice, P5, P2 tog: 27 sts.

Rnd 39{47-51}: (K2 tog, P1) around: 18 sts.

Rnd 40{48-52}: P2 tog around: 9 sts.

Cut yarn leaving an 8" (20.5 cm) length for sewing. Thread tapestry needle with end and slip remaining sts from cord onto needle; remove cord. Pull **tightly** to close and secure end.

3

TRACKS

◖◼▢◻ **EASY**

Sizes

Sizes	Finished Circumference	
Newborn to 3 months	10"	(25.5 cm)
3-6 months	11^1/$_4$"	(28.5 cm)
6-12 months	12^1/$_2$"	(32 cm)

Size Note: Instructions are written for size Newborn to 3 months with sizes 3-6 months and 6-12 months in braces { }. Instructions will be easier to read if you circle all the numbers pertaining to your baby's size. If only one number is given, it applies to all sizes.

MATERIALS

Light Weight Yarn 🔵 **3** LIGHT
[5 ounces, 395 yards
(140 grams, 361 meters) per skein]:
   1 skein
Knook, size G (4 mm) **or** size needed for gauge
Split-ring marker
Tapestry needle

GAUGE: In pattern, 18 sts = 3^3/$_4$" (9.5 cm)

Techniques used:
• YO (*Fig. 6a, page 28*)
• K2 tog (*Figs. 7a & b, page 28*)

HAT

Ch 47{53-59} sts.

Foundation Rnd (Right side)**:** Bring first ch around to meet last ch made, making sure that the ch isn't twisted and pick up a st in the first ch and in each ch around *(see Circular Knitting, page 26)*. Place split-ring marker around first st to indicate the beginning of the rnd: 48{54-60} sts.

Rnd 1: Purl around.

Rnd 2: Knit around.

Rnds 3-5: Repeat Rnds 1 and 2 once, then repeat Rnd 1 once **more**.

Rnd 6: K3, K2 tog, (YO, K4, K2 tog) around to last st, YO, K1.

On the round following a yarn over, you must be careful to treat it as a stitch by knitting it.

Rnd 7: Knit around.

Rnd 8: K2, K2 tog, (YO, K4, K2 tog) around to last 2 sts, YO, K2.

Rnd 9: Knit around.

Rnd 10: K1, K2 tog, (YO, K4, K2 tog) around to last 3 sts, YO, K3.

Rnd 11: Knit around.

Rnd 12: (K2 tog, YO, K4) around.

Rnd 13: Knit around to last st, work last st as part of next rnd.

Rnd 14: K2 tog, move marker to st just made, YO, K4, (K2 tog, YO, K4) around.

Rnd 15: K2, move marker to last st made, knit around.

Rnd 16: (K4, K2 tog, YO) around.

Rnd 17: Knit around.

Rnds 18-29: Repeat Rnds 6-17.

Rnds 30-36: Repeat Rnds 6-12.

Rnd 37: Knit around to last 4 sts, K2 tog twice: 52 sts.

Rnd 38: K5, K2 tog, (YO, K4, K2 tog) around to last 3 sts, YO, K3.

Rnd 39: Knit around to last 4 sts, K2 tog twice: 50 sts.

Rnd 40: K4, K2 tog, (YO, K4, K2 tog) around to last 2 sts, YO, K2.

Rnd 41: Knit around to last 4 sts, K2 tog twice: 48 sts.

SIZE 6-12 MONTHS ONLY
Rnds 30-34: Repeat Rnds 6-10.

Rnd 35: K 14, K2 tog, K 28, K2 tog, K 14: 58 sts.

Rnd 36: (K2 tog, YO, K4) twice, K2 tog, YO, K3, (K2 tog, YO, K4) 4 times, K2 tog, YO, K3, (K2 tog, YO, K4) twice.

Rnd 37: K 13, K2 tog, K 27, K2 tog, K 14: 56 sts.

Rnd 38: K5, K2 tog, YO, K4, K2 tog, YO, K2, (K2 tog, YO, K4) 4 times, K2 tog, YO, K2, K2 tog, YO, K4, K2 tog, YO, K5.

Rnd 39: K 12, K2 tog twice, K 24, K2 tog twice, K 12: 52 sts.

Rnd 40: K4, K2 tog, YO, K4, (K2 tog, YO) twice, K4, (K2 tog, YO, K4) 3 times, (K2 tog, YO) twice, (K4, K2 tog, YO) twice.

Rnd 41: K 11, K2 tog twice, K 22, K2 tog twice, K 11: 48 sts.

ALL SIZES
Rnd 30{42-42}: K3, K2 tog, (YO, K4, K2 tog) around to last st, YO, K1.

Rnd 31{43-43}: K 13, K2 tog, K 18, K2 tog, K 13: 46 sts.

Rnd 32{44-44}: K2, K2 tog, YO, K4, K2 tog, YO, K3, (K2 tog, YO, K4) 3 times, K2 tog, YO, K3, K2 tog, YO, K4, K2 tog, YO, K2.

Rnd 33{45-45}: K 10, K2 tog twice, K 18, K2 tog twice, K 10: 42 sts.

Rnd 34{46-46}: K1, K2 tog, YO, K4, K2 tog, YO, K1, (K2 tog, YO, K4) 3 times, K2 tog, YO, K1, K2 tog, YO, K4, K2 tog, YO, K3.

Rnd 35{47-47}: K8, K2 tog twice, K 18, K2 tog twice, K8: 38 sts.

Rnd 36{48-48}: K2 tog, YO, K4, K2 tog, YO, K5, (K2 tog, YO, K4) twice, K2 tog, YO, K5, K2 tog, YO, K4.

Rnd 37{49-49}: K7, K2 tog twice, K 16, K2 tog twice, K7: 34 sts.

Rnd 38{50-50}: K6, (K2 tog, K2) around: 27 sts.

Rnd 39{51-51}: (K2 tog, K1) around: 18 sts.

Rnd 40{52-52}: K2 tog around: 9 sts.

Cut yarn leaving an 8" (20.5 cm) length for sewing. Thread tapestry needle with end and slip remaining sts from cord onto needle; remove cord. Pull **tightly** to close and secure end.

DOUBLE DIAMONDS

●■□□ EASY +

Sizes

Sizes	Finished Circumference	
Newborn to 3 months	10"	(25.5 cm)
3-6 months	12"	(30.5 cm)
6-12 months	14"	(35.5 cm)

Size Note: Instructions are written for size Newborn to 3 months with sizes 3-6 months and 6-12 months in braces { }. Instructions will be easier to read if you circle all the numbers pertaining to your baby's size. If only one number is given, it applies to all sizes.

MATERIALS

Light Weight Yarn **3 LIGHT**
[5 ounces, 395 yards
(140 grams, 361 meters) per skein]:
   1 skein
Knook, size G (4 mm) **or** size needed for gauge
Marker
Tapestry needle

GAUGE: In pattern, 20 sts = 4" (10 cm)

Techniques used:
• K2 tog (*Figs. 7a & b, page 28*)
• Slip 1 as if to **knit**, K1, PSSO (*Fig. 9, page 29*)
• P2 tog (*Fig. 12, page 29*)

HAT
Ch 49{59-69} sts.

Foundation Rnd (Right side)**:** Bring first ch around to meet last ch made, making sure that the ch isn't twisted and pick up a st in the first ch and in each ch around (*see Circular Knitting, page 26*). Place a marker to indicate the beginning of the rnd: 50{60-70} sts.

Rnd 1: Purl around.

Rnd 2: Knit around.

Rnds 3-5: Repeat Rnds 1 and 2 once, then repeat Rnd 1 once **more**.

Rnd 6: ★ K1, P1, (K3, P1) twice; repeat from ★ around.

Rnd 7: P1, K3, P1, K1, P1, ★ (K3, P1) twice, K1, P1; repeat from ★ around to last 3 sts, K3.

Rnd 8: K3, P1, (K1, P1) twice, ★ K5, P1, (K1, P1) twice; repeat from ★ around to last 2 sts, K2.

Rnd 9: K2, P1, (K1, P1) 3 times, ★ K3, P1, (K1, P1) 3 times; repeat from ★ around to last st, K1.

Rnd 10: K3, P1, (K1, P1) twice, ★ K5, P1, (K1, P1) twice; repeat from ★ around to last 2 sts, K2.

Rnd 11: P1, K3, P1, K1, P1, ★ (K3, P1) twice, K1, P1; repeat from ★ around to last 3 sts, K3.

Rnd 12: ★ K1, P1, (K3, P1) twice; repeat from ★ around.

Rnd 13: P1, K1, P1, K5, P1, ★ (K1, P1) twice, K5, P1; repeat from ★ around to last st, K1.

Rnd 14: (K1, P1) twice, K3, P1, ★ (K1, P1) 3 times, K3, P1; repeat from ★ around to last 2 sts, K1, P1.

Rnd 15: P1, K1, P1, K5, P1, ★ (K1, P1) twice, K5, P1; repeat from ★ around to last st, K1.

Rnds 16-35: Repeat Rnds 6-15 twice.

SIZES 3-6 AND 6-12 MONTHS ONLY

Rnd 36: ★ K1, P1, (K3, P1) twice; repeat from ★ around.

Rnd 37: P2 tog, K2, P1, K1, P1, ★ (K3, P1) twice, K1, P1; repeat from ★ around to last 3 sts, K1, slip 1 as if to **knit**, K1, PSSO: {58-68} sts.

Rnd 38: K2, P1, (K1, P1) twice, ★ K5, P1, (K1, P1) twice; repeat from ★ around to last st, K1.

Rnd 39: P2 tog, ★ (K1, P1) 3 times, K3, P1; repeat from ★ around to last 6 sts, (K1, P1) twice, slip 1 as if to **knit**, K1, PSSO: {56-66} sts.

Rnd 40: (K1, P1) 3 times, ★ K5, P1, (K1, P1) twice; repeat from ★ around.

Rnd 41: K2 tog, P1, K1, ★ P1, (K3, P1) twice, K1; repeat from ★ around to last 2 sts, P2 tog: {54-64} sts.

Rnd 42: K2, P1, K3, P1, K1, P1, ★ (K3, P1) twice, K1, P1; repeat from ★ around to last 5 sts, K3, P1, K1.

Rnd 43: K2 tog, K3, P1, (K1, P1) twice, ★ K5, P1, (K1, P1) twice; repeat from ★ around to last 4 sts, K2, slip 1 as if to **knit**, K1, PSSO: {52-62} sts.

Rnd 44: ★ K3, P1, (K1, P1) 3 times; repeat from ★ around to last 2 sts, K2.

Rnd 45: K2 tog, K2, P1, (K1, P1) twice, ★ K5, P1, (K1, P1) twice; repeat from ★ around to last 3 sts, K1, slip 1 as if to **knit**, K1, PSSO: {50-60} sts.

Rnd 46: K4, P1, K1, P1, ★ (K3, P1) twice, K1, P1; repeat from ★ around to last 3 sts, K3.

Rnd 47: K2 tog, ★ (K3, P1) twice, K1, P1; repeat from ★ around to last 8 sts, K3, P1, K2, slip 1 as if to **knit**, K1, PSSO: 58 sts.

Rnd 48: K7, P1, (K1, P1) twice, ★ K5, P1, (K1, P1) twice; repeat from ★ around to last 6 sts, K6.

Rnd 49: K2 tog, K4, ★ P1, (K1, P1) 3 times, K3; repeat from ★ around to last 2 sts, slip 1 as if to **knit**, K1, PSSO: 56 sts.

Rnd 50: K6, ★ P1, (K1, P1) twice, K5; repeat from ★ around.

Rnd 51: K2 tog, K1, P1, K3, P1, K1, P1, ★ (K3, P1) twice, K1, P1; repeat from ★ around to last 6 sts, K3, P1, slip 1 as if to **knit**, K1, PSSO: 54 sts.

Rnd 52: (K1, P1) twice, ★ (K3, P1) twice, K1, P1; repeat from ★ around.

Rnd 53: K2 tog, P1, K1, P1, K5, P1, ★ (K1, P1) twice, K5, P1; repeat from ★ around to last 3 sts, K1, P2 tog: 52 sts.

Rnd 54: P1, (K1, P1) twice, K3, ★ P1, (K1, P1) 3 times, K3; repeat from ★ around to last 4 sts, (P1, K1) twice.

Rnd 55: P2 tog, K1, P1, K5, P1, ★ (K1, P1) twice, K5, P1; repeat from ★ around to last 2 sts, slip 1 as if to **knit**, K1, PSSO: 50 sts.

ALL SIZES

Rnd 36{46-56}: (K8, K2 tog) around: 45 sts.

Rnd 37{47-57}: (P7, P2 tog) around: 40 sts.

Rnd 38{48-58}: (K6, K2 tog) around: 35 sts.

Rnd 39{49-59}: P3, (P2 tog, P2) around: 27 sts.

Rnd 40{50-60}: (K2 tog, K1) around: 18 sts.

Rnd 41{51-61}: P2 tog around: 9 sts.

Cut yarn leaving an 8" (20.5 cm) length for sewing. Thread tapestry needle with end and slip remaining sts from cord onto needle; remove cord. Pull **tightly** to close and secure end.

DOUGHNUTS

◀■■■▭ **INTERMEDIATE**

Sizes

Sizes	Finished Circumference
Newborn to 3 months	10" (25.5 cm)
3-6 months	11^1/$_4$" (28.5 cm)
6-12 months	12^1/$_2$" (32 cm)

Size Note: Instructions are written for size Newborn to 3 months with sizes 3-6 months and 6-12 months in braces { }. Instructions will be easier to read if you circle all the numbers pertaining to your baby's size. If only one number is given, it applies to all sizes.

MATERIALS

Light Weight Yarn 🧶 **3**
[5 ounces, 395 yards
(140 grams, 361 meters) per skein]:
  1 skein
Knook, size G (4 mm) **or** size needed for gauge
Marker
Tapestry needle

GAUGE: In pattern, 5 repeats (25 sts) = 3^1/$_2$" (9 cm)

Techniques used:
• Knit increase *(Figs. 4a & b, page 27)*
• YO *(Fig. 6a, page 28)*
• K2 tog *(Figs. 7a & b, page 28)*
• wyib slip 1 as if to **knit**, K2, PSSO2 *(Fig. 10, page 29)*
• P2 tog *(Fig. 12, page 29)*

HAT
Ch 55{65-75} sts.

Foundation Rnd (Right side): Bring first ch around to meet last ch made, making sure that the ch isn't twisted and pick up a st in the first ch and in each ch around *(see Circular Knitting, page 26)*. Place a marker to indicate the beginning of the rnd: 56{66-76} sts.

Rnds 1-4: (K1, P1) around.

Size Newborn to 3 Months Only - Rnd 5: (Knit increase, K3) around: 70 sts.

Size 3-6 Months Only - Rnd 5: (Knit increase, K3) twice, (knit increase, K4) 10 times, (knit increase, K3) twice: 80 sts.

Size 6-12 Months Only - Rnd 5: (Knit increase, K4) 4 times, (knit increase, K5) 6 times, (knit increase, K4) 4 times: 90 sts.

All Sizes - Rnd 6 (Decrease rnd): ★ P2, wyib slip 1 as if to **knit**, K2, PSSO2; repeat from ★ around: 56{64-72} sts.

Rnd 7 (Increase rnd): (P2, K1, YO, K1) around: 70{80-90} sts.

On the round following a yarn over, you must be careful to treat it as a stitch by knitting it.

Rnds 8 and 9: (P2, K3) around.

Rnds 10-34: Repeat Rnds 6-9, 6 times; then repeat Rnd 6 once **more**: 56{64-72} sts.

SIZE 6-12 MONTHS ONLY
Rnd 35: (P2, K1, YO, K1) 5 times, P2, K2, (P2, K1, YO, K1) 6 times, P2, K2, (P2, K1, YO, K1) 5 times: 88 sts.

Rnd 36: (P2, K3) 5 times, P2 tog, K2 tog, (P2, K3) 6 times, P2 tog, K2 tog, (P2, K3) 5 times: 84 sts.

Rnd 37: ★ (P2, K3) 5 times, P2 tog twice, K3; repeat from ★ once **more**, (P2, K3) 4 times: 80 sts.

Rnd 38: ★ P2, wyib slip 1 as if to **knit**, K2, PSSO2; repeat from ★ around: 64 sts.

SIZES 3-6 AND 6-12 MONTHS ONLY
Rnd {35-39}: (P2, K1, YO, K1) 4 times, P2, K2, (P2, K1, YO, K1) 6 times, P2, K2, (P2, K1, YO, K1) 4 times: 78 sts.

Rnd {36-40}: (P2, K3) 4 times, P2 tog, K2 tog, (P2, K3) 6 times, P2 tog, K2 tog, (P2, K3) 4 times: 74 sts.

Rnd {37-41}: (P2, K3) 4 times, P2 tog twice, K3, (P2, K3) 5 times, P2 tog twice, K3, (P2, K3) 3 times: 70 sts.

Rnd {38-42}: ★ P2, wyib slip 1 as if to **knit**, K2, PSSO2; repeat from ★ around: 56 sts.

ALL SIZES
Rnd 35{39-43}: (P2, K2) around.

Rnd 36{40-44}: (P2 tog, K2) around: 42 sts.

Rnd 37{41-45}: (P1, K2, P1, K2 tog) around: 35 sts.

Rnd 38{42-46}: K3, (K2 tog, K2) around: 27 sts.

Rnd 39{43-47}: (K1, K2 tog) around: 18 sts.

Rnd 40{44-48}: K2 tog around: 9 sts.

Cut yarn leaving an 8" (20.5 cm) length for sewing. Thread tapestry needle with end and slip remaining sts from cord onto needle; remove cord. Pull **tightly** to close and secure end.

LACE DIAMONDS

Shown on page 16.

◼◼◼◻ **INTERMEDIATE**

Sizes	Finished Circumference
Newborn to 3 months	10¹/₂" (26.5 cm)
3-6 months	12¹/₄" (31 cm)
6-12 months	14" (35.5 cm)

Size Note: Instructions are written for size Newborn to 3 months with sizes 3-6 months and 6-12 months in braces { }. Instructions will be easier to read if you circle all the numbers pertaining to your baby's size. If only one number is given, it applies to all sizes.

MATERIALS

Light Weight Yarn **3** LIGHT
[5 ounces, 395 yards
(140 grams, 361 meters) per skein]:
    1 skein
Knook, size G (4 mm) **or** size needed for gauge
Marker
Tapestry needle

GAUGE: In pattern,
        3 repeats (24 sts) = 5¹/₄" (13.25 cm)

Techniques used:
• YO *(Fig. 6a, page 28)*
• K2 tog *(Figs. 7a & b, page 28)*
• K2 tog tbl *(Fig. 8, page 28)*
• Slip 1 as if to **knit**, K2 tog, PSSO *(Fig. 11, page 29)*
• P2 tog *(Fig. 12, page 29)*

HAT

Ch 47{55-63} sts.

Foundation Rnd (Right side)**:** Bring first ch around to meet last ch made, making sure that the ch isn't twisted and pick up a st in the first ch and in each ch around *(see Circular Knitting, page 26)*. Place a marker to indicate the beginning of the rnd: 48{56-64} sts.

Rnd 1: Purl around.

Rnd 2: Knit around.

Rnds 3-5: Repeat Rnds 1 and 2 once, then repeat Rnd 1 once **more**.

Rnd 6: K4, K2 tog, ★ YO, K6, K2 tog; repeat from ★ around to last 2 sts, YO, K2.

On the round following a yarn over, you must be careful to treat it as a stitch by knitting it.

Rnd 7 AND ALL ODD NUMBERED RNDS thru Rnd 37: Knit around.

Rnd 8: ★ K3, K2 tog, YO, K1, YO, K2 tog tbl; repeat from ★ around.

Rnd 10: ★ K2 tog tbl, K1, K2 tog, YO, K3, YO; repeat from ★ around.

Rnd 12: ★ YO, slip 1 as if to **knit**, K2 tog, PSSO, YO, K5; repeat from ★ around.

Rnd 14: ★ K2 tog, YO, K6; repeat from ★ around.

Rnd 16: ★ YO, K1, YO, K2 tog tbl, K3, K2 tog; repeat from ★ around.

Rnd 18: ★ K3, YO, K2 tog tbl, K1, K2 tog, YO; repeat from ★ around.

Rnd 20: K4, YO, slip 1 as if to **knit**, K2 tog, PSSO, YO, ★ K5, YO, slip 1 as if to **knit**, K2 tog, PSSO, YO; repeat from ★ around to last st, K1.

Rnd 22: K4, K2 tog, ★ YO, K6, K2 tog; repeat from ★ around to last 2 sts, YO, K2.

Rnds 23-38: Repeat Rnds 7-22.

SIZE NEWBORN TO 3 MONTHS ONLY
Rnd 39: Knit around.

SIZE 3-6 MONTHS ONLY
Rnds 39-44: Repeat Rnds 7-12.

Rnd 45: K2 tog tbl twice, knit around to last 4 sts, K2 tog twice: 52 sts.

Rnd 46: ★ K6, K2 tog, YO; repeat from ★ around to last 4 sts, K4.

Rnd 47: K2 tog tbl twice, knit around to last 4 sts, K2 tog twice: 48 sts.

SIZE 6-12 MONTHS ONLY
Rnds 39-44: Repeat Rnds 7-12.

Rnd 45: K2 tog tbl twice, knit around to last 4 sts, K2 tog twice: 60 sts.

Rnd 46: ★ K6, K2 tog, YO; repeat from ★ around to last 4 sts, K4.

Rnd 47: K2 tog tbl twice, knit around to last 4 sts, K2 tog twice: 56 sts.

Rnd 48: ★ K3, K2 tog, YO, K1, YO, K2 tog tbl; repeat from ★ around.

Rnd 49: K2 tog tbl, knit around to last 2 sts, K2 tog: 54 sts.

Rnd 50: K1, K2 tog, YO, K3, ★ YO, K2 tog tbl, K1, K2 tog, YO, K3; repeat from ★ around.

Rnd 51: K2 tog tbl, knit around to last 2 sts, K2 tog: 52 sts.

Rnd 52: K6, YO, slip 1 as if to **knit**, K2 tog, PSSO, ★ YO, K5, YO, slip 1 as if to **knit**, K2 tog, PSSO; repeat from ★ around to last 3 sts, YO, K3.

Rnd 53: K2 tog tbl, knit around to last 2 sts, K2 tog: 50 sts.

Rnd 54: K5, K2 tog, ★ YO, K6, K2 tog; repeat from ★ around to last 3 sts, YO, K3.

Rnd 55: K2 tog tbl, knit around to last 2 sts, K2 tog: 48 sts.

ALL SIZES
Rnd 40{48-56}: (P4, P2 tog) around: 40 sts.

Rnd 41{49-57}: (K3, K2 tog) around: 32 sts.

Rnd 42{50-58}: (P2, P2 tog) around: 24 sts.

Rnd 43{51-59}: (K1, K2 tog) around: 16 sts.

Rnd 44{52-60}: P2 tog around: 8 sts.

Cut yarn leaving an 8" (20.5 cm) length for sewing. Thread tapestry needle with end and slip remaining sts from cord onto needle; remove cord. Pull **tightly** to close and secure end.

WAVES

INTERMEDIATE

Sizes

Sizes	Finished Circumference	
Newborn to 3 months	10"	(25.5 cm)
3-6 months	12¹/₂"	(32 cm)
6-12 months	15"	(38 cm)

Size Note: Instructions are written for size Newborn to 3 months with sizes 3-6 months and 6-12 months in braces { }. Instructions will be easier to read if you circle all the numbers pertaining to your baby's size. If only one number is given, it applies to all sizes.

MATERIALS

Light Weight Yarn

[4 ounces, 360 yards
(113 grams, 329 meters) per skein]:
    1 skein
Knook, size G (4 mm) **or** size needed for gauge
Marker
Tapestry needle

GAUGE: In pattern,
        2 repeats (24 sts) = 5" (12.75 cm)

Techniques used:
• YO *(Fig. 6b, page 28)*
• K2 tog *(Figs. 7a & b, page 28)*
• P2 tog *(Fig. 12, page 29)*

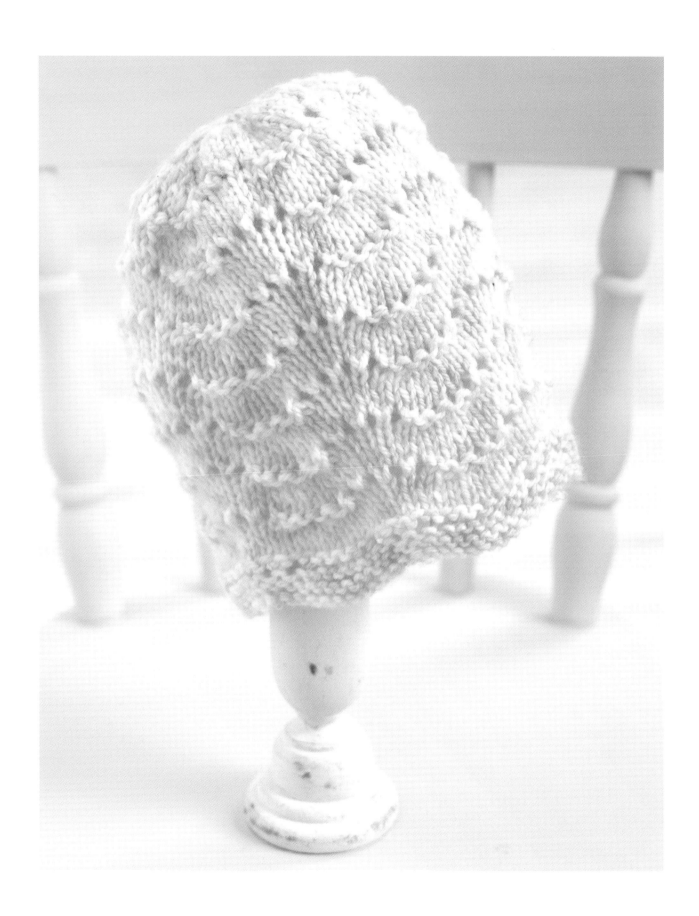

HAT

Ch 47{59-71} sts.

Foundation Rnd (Right side)**:** Bring first ch around to meet last ch made, making sure that the ch isn't twisted and pick up a st in the first ch and in each ch around *(see Circular Knitting, page 26)*. Place a marker to indicate the beginning of the rnd: 48{60-72} sts.

Rnd 1: Purl around.

Rnd 2: Knit around.

Rnds 3 and 4: Repeat Rnds 1 and 2.

Rnd 5: P2 tog twice, (P1, YO) 4 times, ★ P2 tog 4 times, (P1, YO) 4 times; repeat from ★ around to last 4 sts, P2 tog twice.

On the round following a yarn over, you must be careful to treat it as a stitch by knitting it.

Rnds 6-10: Knit around.

Rnds 11 thru 35{41-47}: Repeat Rnds 5-10, 4{5-6} times; then repeat Rnd 5 once **more**.

SIZE 3-6 MONTHS ONLY

Rnd 42: K2 tog, K 12, K2 tog twice, K 24, K2 tog twice, K 12, K2 tog: 54 sts.

Rnd 43: K2 tog, K 12, K2 tog twice, K 16, K2 tog twice, K 14, K2 tog: 48 sts.

SIZE 6-12 MONTHS ONLY

Rnd 48: K2 tog, K 16, K2 tog twice, K 28, K2 tog twice, K 16, K2 tog: 66 sts.

Rnd 49: K2 tog, K 16, K2 tog twice, K 20, K2 tog twice, K 18, K2 tog: 60 sts.

Rnd 50: K2 tog, K 12, K2 tog twice, K 24, K2 tog twice, K 12, K2 tog: 54 sts.

Rnd 51: K2 tog, K 12, K2 tog twice, K 16, K2 tog twice, K 14, K2 tog: 48 sts.

ALL SIZES

Rnd 36{44-52}: K2 tog, K8, K2 tog twice, K 20, K2 tog twice, K8, K2 tog: 42 sts.

Rnd 37{45-53}: K2 tog, K9, K2 tog twice, K 13, K2 tog twice, K8, K2 tog: 36 sts.

Rnd 38{46-54}: (K2 tog, K2) around: 27 sts.

Rnd 39{47-55}: (K2 tog, K1) around: 18 sts.

Rnd 40{48-56}: K2 tog around: 9 sts.

Cut yarn leaving an 8" (20.5 cm) length for sewing. Thread tapestry needle with end and slip remaining sts from cord onto needle; remove cord. Pull **tightly** to close and secure end.

MARBLES

Shown on page 22.

Sizes	Finished Circumference	
Newborn to 3 months	9¹/₄"	(23.5 cm)
3-6 months	11¹/₄"	(28.5 cm)
6-12 months	13¹/₄"	(33.5 cm)

Size Note: Instructions are written for size Newborn to 3 months with sizes 3-6 months and 6-12 months in braces { }. Instructions will be easier to read if you circle all the numbers pertaining to your baby's size. If only one number is given, it applies to all sizes.

MATERIALS

Light Weight Yarn (**LIGHT 3**)
[5 ounces, 395 yards
(140 grams, 361 meters) per skein]:
   1 skein
Knook, size G (4 mm) **or** size needed for gauge
Marker
Tapestry needle

GAUGE: In pattern, 6 repeats (24 sts) = 4" (10 cm)

Techniques used:
• Double increase *(Fig. 5, page 27)*
• K2 tog *(Figs. 7a & b, page 28)*
• P3 tog *(Figs. 13a & b, page 29)*

Hat is worked with **wrong** side facing throughout.

HAT

Ch 55{67-79} sts.

Foundation Rnd (Wrong side)**:** Bring first ch around to meet last ch made, making sure that the ch isn't twisted and pick up a st in the first ch and in each ch around *(see Circular Knitting, page 26)*. Place a marker to indicate the beginning of the rnd: 56{68-80} sts.

Rnds 1-5: (K1, P1) around.

Rnd 6: Knit around.

Rnd 7: (Double increase, P3 tog) around.

Rnd 8: Knit around.

Rnd 9: (P3 tog, double increase) around.

Rnds 10 thru 25{29-29}: Repeat Rnds 6-9, 4{5-5} times.

SIZE 6-12 MONTHS ONLY

Rnd 30: K 16, K2 tog twice, K 36, K2 tog twice, K 16, K2 tog twice: 74 sts.

Rnd 31: (Double increase, P3 tog) 4 times, K2, (double increase, P3 tog) 9 times, K2, (double increase, P3 tog) 4 times, K2.

Rnd 32: K 16, K2 tog twice, K 32, K2 tog twice, K 14, K2 tog twice: 68 sts.

Rnd 33: (P3 tog, double increase) around.

SIZES 3-6 AND 6-12 MONTHS ONLY

Rnd {30-34}: K 12, K2 tog twice, K 32, K2 tog twice, K 12, K2 tog twice: 62 sts.

Rnd {31-35}: (Double increase, P3 tog) 3 times, K2, (double increase, P3 tog) 8 times, K2, (double increase, P3 tog) 3 times, K2.

Rnd {32-36}: K 12, K2 tog twice, K 28, K2 tog twice, K 10, K2 tog twice: 56 sts.

Rnd {33-37}: (P3 tog, double increase) around.

ALL SIZES

Rnd 26{34-38}: K 12, K2 tog twice, K 24, K2 tog twice, K 12: 52 sts.

Rnd 27{35-39}: (Double increase, P3 tog) 3 times, K2, (double increase, P3 tog) 6 times, K2, (double increase, P3 tog) 3 times.

Rnd 28{36-40}: K 11, K2 tog twice, K 22, K2 tog twice, K 11: 48 sts.

Rnd 29{37-41}: (P3 tog, double increase) around.

Rnd 30{38-42}: K8, K2 tog twice, K 20, K2 tog twice, K 12: 44 sts.

Rnd 31{39-43}: (Double increase, P3 tog) twice, K2, (double increase, P3 tog) 5 times, K2, (double increase, P3 tog) 3 times.

Rnd 32{40-44}: K7, K2 tog twice, K 18, K2 tog twice, K 11: 40 sts.

Rnd 33{41-45}: (P3 tog, double increase) around.

Rnd 34{42-46}: K2 tog, K2, (K2 tog twice, K2) around: 27 sts.

Rnd 35{43-47}: (K2 tog, K1) around: 18 sts.

Rnd 36{44-48}: K2 tog around: 9 sts.

Cut yarn leaving an 8" (20.5 cm) length for sewing. Thread tapestry needle with end and slip remaining sts from cord onto needle; remove cord. Pull **tightly** to close and secure end.

GENERAL INSTRUCTIONS

ABBREVIATIONS

ch(s)	chain(s)
cm	centimeters
K	knit
mm	millimeters
P	purl
PSSO	pass slipped st(s) over
PSSO2	pass slipped st over 2
Rnd(s)	Round(s)
sts(s)	stitches
tbl	through back loops
tog	together
wyib	with yarn in back
YO	yarn over

★ — work instructions following ★ as many **more** times as indicated in addition to the first time.

( ) or [ ] — work enclosed instructions **as many** times as specified by the number immediately following **or** work all enclosed instructions in the stitch or space indicated **or** contains explanatory remarks.

colon (:) — the number(s) given after a colon at the end of a round denotes the number of stitches you should have on that round.

front vs. **back** side — as you are working, the side facing you is the **front** of your work; the **back** is the side away from you.

right vs. **wrong** side — on the finished piece, the right side of your work is the side the public will see.

KNOOK TERMINOLOGY		
UNITED STATES		**INTERNATIONAL**
gauge	=	tension
bind off	=	cast off
yarn over (YO)	=	yarn forward (yfwd) **or** yarn around needle (yrn)

KNOOK TIP

When using Light Weight Yarn, it may be easier to work the stitches and also to pull the cord through the stitches just made if you substitute a thinner cord for the cord that comes with the Knook. Crochet cotton size 10 thread works well.

GAUGE

Gauge is the number of stitches and rows in every inch of your knitted piece. Exact gauge is essential for proper size. Before beginning your project, make a sample swatch using the yarn and Knook specified in the individual instructions. After completing the swatch, measure it, counting your stitches and rows carefully. If your swatch is larger or smaller than specified, make another, changing Knook size to get the correct gauge. Keep trying until you find the size Knook that will give you the specified gauge.

Yarn Weight Symbol & Names	SUPER FINE 1	FINE 2	LIGHT 3	MEDIUM 4	BULKY 5	SUPER BULKY 6
Type of Yarns in Category	Sock, Fingering Baby	Sport, Baby	DK, Light Worsted	Worsted, Afghan, Aran	Chunky, Craft, Rug	Bulky, Roving
Knook Gauge Ranges in Stockinette St to 4" (10 cm)	27-32 sts	23-26 sts	21-24 sts	16-20 sts	12-15 sts	6-11 sts
Advised Knook Size Range	B-1 to D-3	D-3 to F-5	F-5 to G-6	G-6 to I-9	I-9 to K-10½	M-13 and larger

■□□□ BEGINNER	Projects for first-time stitchers using basic knit and purl stitches. Minimal shaping.
■■□□ EASY	Projects using basic stitches, repetitive stitch patterns, simple color changes, knitting in the round techniques, and simple shaping and finishing.
■■■□ INTERMEDIATE	Projects with a variety of stitches, such as basic cables and lace, simple intarsia, and mid-level shaping and finishing.
■■■■ EXPERIENCED	Projects using advanced techniques and stitches, such as short rows, fair isle, more intricate intarsia, cables, lace patterns, and numerous color changes.

CIRCULAR KNITTING

When you knit a tube, as for a hat, you are going to work around and around on the outside of the circle with the right side of the knitting facing you.

If your hat is worked in Stockinette Stitch, you have eliminated having to work any purl rows, and you will knit every round. If your hat is worked in Garter Stitch, you will alternate one knit round with one purl round.

To begin working in the round, chain the number called for in your project.

Bring the first chain around to meet the last chain made, making sure that the chain isn't twisted (**Fig. 1a**).

Fig. 1a

Begin by picking up a stitch in the first chain (**Fig. 1b**) and in each chain around. Remember that the loop on the Knook counts as your first stitch.

Fig. 1b

Before beginning your first round, place a ring marker on the Knook before the first stitch to mark the beginning of the round (**Fig. 1c**), **or** place a split-ring marker around the first stitch to indicate the beginning of the round.

Fig. 1c

You can slide the cord out of the stitches as you work or after each round is complete.

THROUGH BACK LOOP
(abbreviated tbl)

When instructed to knit or purl into the back loop of a stitch (**Fig. 2**), the result will be twisted stitches. To knit through the back loop, with yarn in back, insert Knook into back of the stitch from **front** to **back**.

Fig. 2

SLIP 1

Insert the Knook into next stitch as if to **knit** (*Fig. 3a*) or as if to **purl** (*Fig. 3b*) as specified.

Fig. 3a

Fig. 3b

KNIT INCREASE

Knit the next stitch (*Fig. 4a*), then knit into the **back** loop of the **same** stitch (*Fig. 4b*).

Fig. 4a

Fig. 4b

DOUBLE INCREASE

Knit the next stitch, then purl **and** knit into the **same** stitch (*Fig. 5*).

Fig. 5

YARN OVER (abbreviated YO)

A yarn over is simply placing the yarn over the Knook creating an extra stitch. Since the yarn over produces a hole in the knit fabric, it is used for a lacy effect. On the row following a yarn over, you must be careful to treat it as a stitch by knitting or purling it as instructed.

When a YO is **between 2 knit stitches:**
Bring the yarn to the front **under** the Knook, then back **over** the top of the Knook, so that it is in position for you to knit the next stitch (**Fig. 6a**).

Fig. 6a

When a YO is **between 2 purl stitches**:
Bring the yarn **over** the Knook to the back, then forward **under** the Knook so that it is in position for you to purl the next stitch (**Fig. 6b**).

Fig. 6b

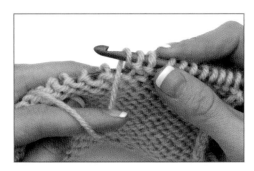

DECREASES
KNIT 2 TOGETHER (abbreviated K2 tog)

Insert the Knook into the **front** of the second and then the first stitch on the cord as if to **knit** (**Fig. 7a**), then **knit** them together as if they were one stitch (**Fig. 7b**).

Fig. 7a

Fig. 7b

KNIT 2 TOGETHER THROUGH BACK LOOP (abbreviated K2 tog tbl)

Insert the Knook into the next two stitches as if to **purl** (**Fig. 8**), then **knit** them together as if they were one stitch.

Fig. 8

SLIP 1, KNIT 1, PASS SLIPPED STITCH OVER (abbreviated slip 1, K1, PSSO)

Slip one stitch as if to **knit** (*Fig. 3a, page 27*). Knit the next stitch. Pull the stitch just made through the slipped stitch (*Fig. 9*).

Fig. 9

SLIP 1, KNIT 2, PASS SLIPPED STITCH OVER 2 (abbreviated slip 1, K2, PSSO2)

Slip one stitch as if to **knit** (*Fig. 3a, page 27*). Knit the next 2 stitches. Pull both stitches just made through the slipped stitch (*Fig. 10*).

Fig. 10

SLIP 1, KNIT 2 TOGETHER, PASS SLIPPED STITCH OVER
(abbreviated slip 1, K2 tog, PSSO)

Slip one stitch as if to **knit** (*Fig. 3a, page 27*). Knit the next 2 stitches together (*Figs. 7a & b, page 28*). Pull the stitch just made through the slipped stitch (*Fig. 11*).

Fig. 11

PURL 2 TOGETHER (abbreviated P2 tog)

Insert the Knook into the **front** of the first 2 stitches on the cord as if to **purl** (*Fig. 12*), then **purl** them together as if they were one stitch.

Fig. 12

PURL 3 TOGETHER (abbreviated P3 tog)

Insert the Knook into the **front** of the first 3 stitches on the cord as if to **purl** (*Fig. 13a*), then **purl** them together as if they were one stitch (*Fig. 13b*).

Fig. 13a

Fig. 13b

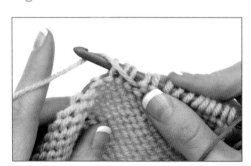

KNOOK BASICS

Using the Knook to create amazing knitted projects is fun and so easy! Let our step-by-step Basic Instructions show you how it's done. They're written and photographed for both left- and right-hand knooking. You'll get off to a fast start and be ready to create any of these beautiful hats. Be sure to visit LeisureArts.com to see the video versions of these instructions—every stitch and technique in this book is there, plus a few more! You'll also find free patterns for more Knook designs!

KNOOK PREP
Thread the cord through the hole at the end of the Knook. Gently pull the cord so that one end is approximately 8" (20.5 cm) from the Knook *(Fig. A)*, leaving a long end.

Fig. A

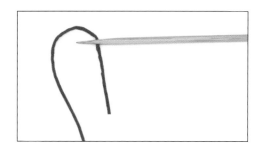

HOLDING THE KNOOK
There are two ways to hold the Knook. Hold the Knook as you would hold a pencil *(Fig. B)*, or as you would grasp a table knife *(Fig. C)*. Find the manner that is most comfortable for you.

Fig. B
Right-handed

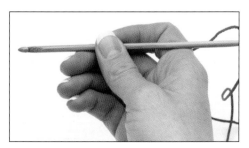

Left-handed

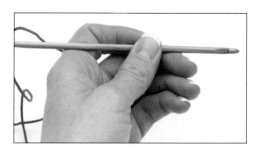

Fig. C
Right-handed

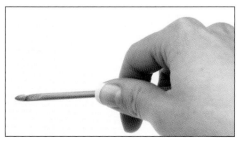

Left-handed

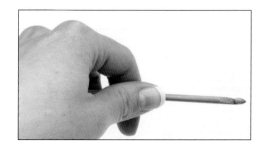

SLIP KNOT

The first step is to make a slip knot. Pull a length of yarn from the skein and make a circle approximately 8" (20.5 cm) from the end and place it on top of the yarn. The yarn on the skein-side of the circle is the working yarn, the opposite end is the yarn tail.

Slip the Knook under the yarn in the center of the circle (*Fig. D*), then pull on both ends to tighten (*Fig. E*).

Fig. D
Right-handed

Left-handed

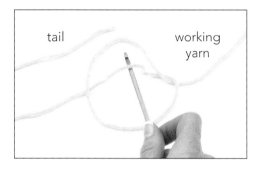

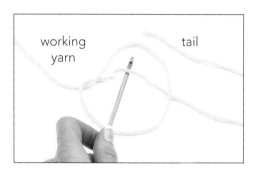

Fig. E
Right-handed

Left-handed

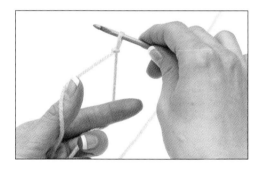

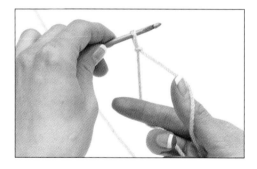

FOUNDATION CHAIN

Once the slip knot is on the Knook, the next step is to chain the required number of stitches, which is called the foundation chain.

With the Knook in your preferred hand, hold the slip knot with your thumb and middle finger of your other hand. Loop the working yarn over your index finger, grasping it in your palm to help control the tension of your yarn as you work the stitches (*Fig. F*).

Fig. F
Right-handed

Left-handed

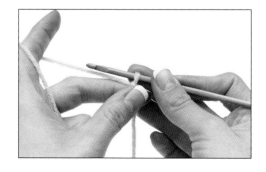

Wrap the yarn around the Knook from **back** to **front** *(Fig. G)*.

Fig. G
Right-handed   Left-handed

   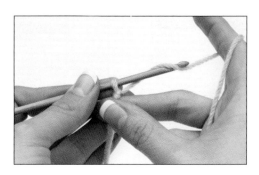

Turn the Knook to catch the yarn and draw the yarn through the slip knot *(Fig. H)*. Each time you wrap the yarn and draw the yarn through, you make one chain *(abbreviated ch)* of the foundation chain.

Fig. H
Right-handed   Left-handed

Repeat these steps to make the required number of chains.

If you already know how to crochet, please study the photos closely. From this point on, you will **NOT** be using the same yarn over typically used in crochet.

PICKING UP STITCHES

The loop on your Knook counts as the first stitch *(abbreviated st)*. To pick up the next stitch, insert the Knook from **front** to **back** into the second chain from the Knook *(Fig. I, page 33)*. With the Knook facing down, catch the yarn *(Fig. J, page 33)* and pull the yarn through the chain *(Fig. K, page 33)*. Repeat until you have picked up a stitch in each chain across *(Fig. L, page 33)*.

Fig. I
Right-handed

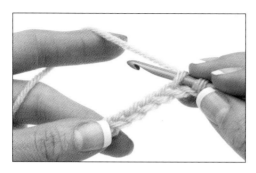

Left-handed

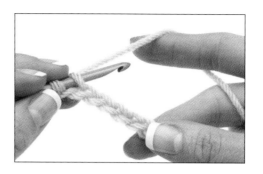

Fig. J
Right-handed

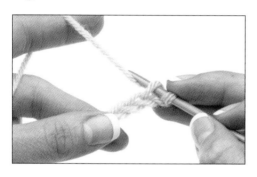

Left-handed

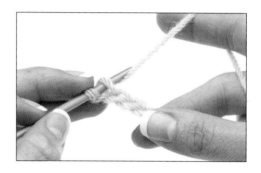

Fig. K
Right-handed

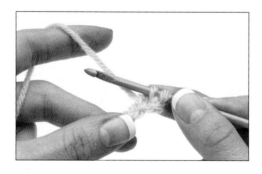

Left-handed

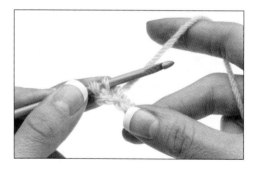

Fig. L
Right-handed

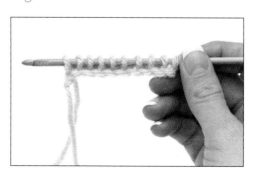

Left-handed

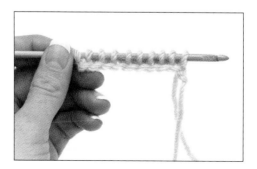

Slide the stitches off the Knook onto the cord *(Fig. M)*, allowing the short end to hang freely *(Fig. N)*.

Fig. M
Right-handed

Left-handed

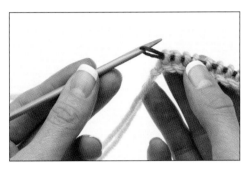

Fig. N
Right-handed

Left-handed

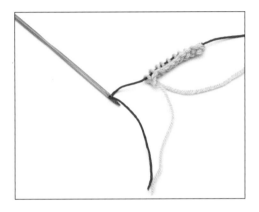

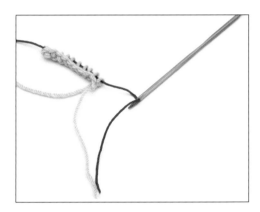

Turn your work around so that the working yarn and the yarn tail are closest to the Knook *(Fig. O)*.

Fig. O
Right-handed

Left-handed

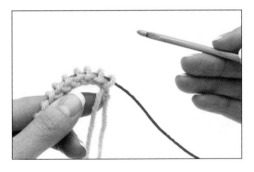

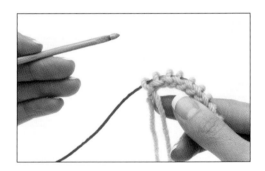

With the Knook in your preferred hand, hold your work with your other hand. Loop the working yarn over your index finger *(Fig. P)*.

Fig. P
Right-handed

Left-handed

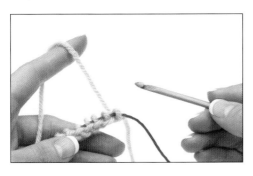
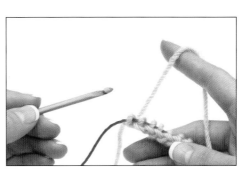

KNIT STITCH

Hold the work with the yarn to the **back**.

For right-handers, insert the Knook from **left** to **right** into the first stitch *(Fig. Q)*.

Fig. Q
Right-handed

For left-handers, insert the Knook from **right** to **left** into the first stitch *(Fig. Q)*.

Fig. Q
Left-handed

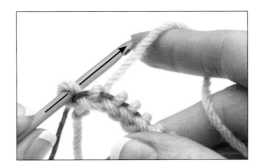

With the Knook facing down, catch the yarn *(Fig. R)* and pull it through the stitch, forming a knit stitch on the Knook *(Fig. S)*.

Fig. R
Right-handed

Left-handed

Fig. S
Right-handed

Left-handed

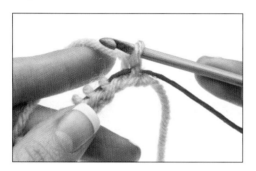
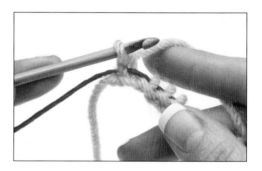

Keeping the yarn to the **back** of your work, repeat this process for each stitch across. Count the stitches to make sure you have the same number of stitches *(Fig. T)*.

Fig. T
Right-handed

Left-handed

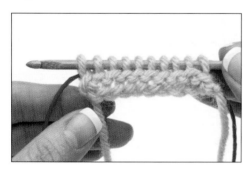

If you do not have the required number of stitches, it is very easy to fix it at this point. Simply pull the Knook back out in the opposite direction you were working until you get to the mistake, and pull the yarn to undo the stitches.

Once each stitch has been worked, gently pull the long end of the cord out of the work, leaving the new stitches on the Knook *(Fig. U)*.

Fig. U
Right-handed

Left-handed

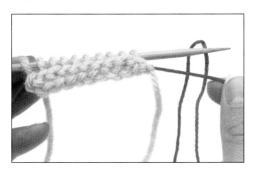
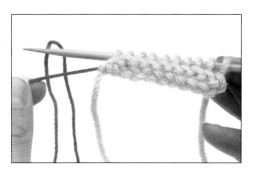

Slide the stitches off the Knook onto the long end of the cord, then turn the work.

PURL STITCH
Hold the work with the yarn to the **front**.

For right-handers, insert the Knook into the stitch from **right** to **left** *(Fig. V)*.

Fig. V
Right-handed

For left-handers, insert the Knook into the stitch from **left** to **right** *(Fig. V)*.

Fig. V
Left-handed

With the Knook facing away from you, wrap the yarn from **front** to **back** (*Fig. W*).

Fig. W
Right-handed

Left-handed

Catch the yarn with the Knook and pull the yarn through the stitch forming a purl stitch on the Knook (*Fig. X*). Keeping the yarn to the **front** of your work, repeat this process for each stitch across the row. Once each stitch has been worked, gently pull the long end of the cord out of the work, leaving the new stitches on the Knook.

Fig. X
Right-handed

Left-handed

Slide the stitches off the Knook onto the long end of the cord, then turn the work.

Working the knit stitch on every row creates a fabric called Garter Stitch. You will also create Garter Stitch if you purl every row.

Garter Stitch

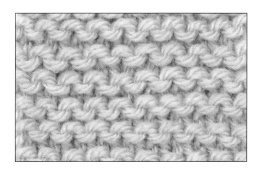

If you alternate knitting one row, then purling one row, the resulting knitted fabric is called Stockinette Stitch.

Stockinette Stitch
(right side)

Stockinette Stitch
(wrong side)

BIND OFF

Binding off is the method used to remove and secure your stitches from the Knook cord so that they won't unravel.

To bind off all the stitches in knit, knit the first two stitches. Pull the second stitch through the first stitch (*Fig. Y*).

Fig. Y
Right-handed

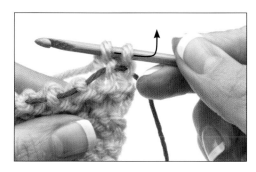

Left-handed

One stitch should remain on the Knook *(Fig. Z)*. Knit the next stitch and pull it through the stitch on the Knook.

Fig. Z
Right-handed

Left-handed

Repeat this process until there are no stitches on the cord and only one stitch remains on the Knook *(Fig. AA)*.

Fig. AA
Right-handed

Left-handed

Pull the cord out of the work. Cut the yarn, leaving a long end to weave in later. Slip the remaining stitch off the Knook, pull the end through the stitch, and tighten the stitch.

To bind off in pattern, knit or purl the first two stitches as indicated for the pattern, pulling the second stitch through the first stitch as illustrated above and continuing across until all stitches are bound off.